Wisdom For The Healing of Nations
A Christian Yogi Writes

WISDOM FOR THE HEALING OF NATIONS

A Christian Yogi Writes

Dr Henry Whitehead
B.M., M.N.I.M.H.

The Book Guild Ltd.
Sussex, England

The Book Guild Ltd.
25 High Street,
Lewes, Sussex.

First published 1991
© Dr Henry Whitehead 1991
Set in Baskerville
Typesetting by APS,
Salisbury, Wiltshire.
Printed in Great Britain by
Antony Rowe Ltd.,
Chippenham, Wiltshire.

British Library Cataloguing in Publication Data
Whitehead, Henry
    Wisdom for the healing of nations.
    1. Mysticism
    I. Title
    294.544
            ISBN 0 86332 608 0

To Marina. Rest in Peace, Love, Joy, Oneness.

'And it shall come to pass in the last days, saith God
I will pour out of my Spirit upon all flesh: and your
sons and you daughters shall prophesy, and your young
men shall see visions, and your old men shall dream dreams . . .'

ACTS 2: Verse 17

About the dust-jacket design:
The sister-Church of that founded by the apostle Thomas in 52 AD on the Malabar Coast of south-west India, graces its crosses with the lotus buds about to blossom. As the text explains, the lotus flower has deep symbolic meanings to those who meditate. The circle makes a mandala to symbolize individuation or Oneness.

CONTENTS

FOREWORD

'And he showed me a pure river of water of
life, clear as crystal, proceeding out of the
throne of God and of the Lamb.'

'In the midst of the street of it and on
either side of the river, was there the tree of
life, which bore twelve manner of fruits,
and yielded her fruit every month: and the
leaves of the tree were for the healing of
nations.'

(Rev. 22 v. 1 and 2)

What kind of person writes a book entitled *Wisdom for the
Healing of Nations*? The same kind of person who says 'Meditation is stilling the mind with love in one's heart in order to
become one with the great, cosmic I AM.' The great, cosmic I
AM is none other than God, a conscious, loving entity who
exists in a state of consciousness which is outside of time, being
reborn in each supreme moment of bliss.

What is a yogi? He or she is a practitioner of yoga. Most
people think of this as simply a form of exercise for the body.
However, the word 'yoga' stems from the same source as 'yoke'.
Yoga is the practice of 'yoking' oneself onto God consciousness.
It is union with God; the supreme mystical experience. The
insights and perceptions of such an experience, which it is
impossible to convey fully in words, have a healing property
which can be applied not only to the individual but to our race
as a whole.

I am convinced that 'The Fall' recorded in Genesis tells the
story of a race of gentle beings, perhaps not unlike the
orangutan, who existed in God consciousness until something
happened to change them into man's present day consciousness, with all our inherent evils. I am also convinced that man
is on the threshold of changing back to the primitive Paradise
state, and that, in the end, we will have no choice in this.

9

However, far from being a curse, it will be the saving of our race.

The states of consciousness I have reached through the practise of yoga have given me a new perception of life. I feel an overwhelming love in my heart for all aspects of our Father's creation, to the extent that the thought of deliberately harming or hurting any part of it unnecessarily, is too repungant to bear. I want everybody to feel this.

In this book I have tried to describe the path through life I am trying to follow. I am a doctor of medicine, not a writer, and I must apologize for my lack of literary skills. I have recorded the insights and perceptions as they have been revealed to me, and are indeed still being revealed to me, thanks be to God.

I dedicate this book to the generations of neo-mystics that are to come. Remember, though, that nothing I have written is new.

Dr Henry Whitehead

INTRODUCTION
and personal viewpoint of
history's most important event
by Dr Henry Whitehead

Two millenia ago a boy was born who was destined to change
the most basic possession of mankind – consciousness itself.
Known as Joshua by his parents and peers, he grew to be
different from them. His enquiring mind led him to spend
much of his childhood alone, in deep thought. He learned to
read quickly and absorbed himself in the only reading matter
available – religious script. This was Israel, a land dominated
by a longstanding religious tradition. The established Church
was highly ordered and exceedingly powerful. If you weren't
seen to be pious by the people of your village you were in for a
hard time. The Rabbis lived and breathed rules, loving to
make a God out of religion.

Joshua was brought up in the church tradition, learning
large passages of religious script each day, to regurgitate to the
Rabbi in order to appease him. In his early teens he became
aware of the hypocrisy and nonsense in what his church forced
on the nation. There was no understanding of the mysteries of
life. Explanations of life, death and their meaning were given as
a verbatim regurgitation of religious script. Anybody who
dared to question this was scolded. Joshua was unhappy at this
stage of life. He could not help think of himself as different from
others. The others in this village eyed him with distrust;
branded him a rebel. Mothers discouraged their sons from
associating with him and his isolation increased. Even his
parents failed to understand. His father, a carpenter, tried
desperately to make him adopt the family trade. He never
stopped telling Joshua how important it was to get along with
other villagers. Any business man knows that he cannot
succeed without goodwill. 'God knows,' he said, 'we're not the
only carpenters in the world. There's plenty of competition.

11

You must get on with them. If you can't accept the Church's ways, pretend that you do.'

From an early age Joshua knew that he was destined for greater things and his quest for understanding of life's mysteries grew. Nobody was really surprised when he announced that he was leaving to travel the world. Many said 'Good riddance'. He was an unsettling influence on what had taken generations to build up.

Travel in those days was a far cry from that of the present day. A real traveller set off for years, or decades, to reach other countries by foot, ox-cart or sailing ship. It was uncertain if he or she would ever see their home or relatives again. However, Joshua wasn't without courage and something deep inside him told him that it was right for him to do. The years that followed led him deep into Asia and Europe. Wherever he went he associated with the wise men, learning the truths found in the already longstanding religions of the World. He learned of Hinduism and the teachings of Gautama, the one called the 'Buddha', of Druidism, or Greek and Roman Gods and much more. He learned that all, or nearly all, religions and philosophies had some truth and that this truth was the essence of all. He found that the Jewish concept of God and life after death were fundamentally wrong. He had been taught of a God that was separate from Mankind; living in a far off heaven; stern and hard; ever ready to punish in anger.

His new teachers told him that God was within; that he and all Mankind were an extension of the great Universal Consciousness in all things. They told him that life was a journey; we start in God; become unaware of His presence for a while and then, once we have developed enough courage, trust and love, become one with Him again. They taught him to still his mind so that the God within could be experienced. This gave him the understanding he craved. From this direct communion with God he found limitless love. He learned that God could not punish in anger; rather that all the pain of life happened for a reason. Without it we would not learn to trust, and without that we could not become one with God, which Joshua found was the heaven beyond description.

Finally, he had found what he was looking for. However, he had to work continuously at maintaining what he had found. This glimpse of God was like a seed within, which he had to

12

continuously feed and water in order for it to grow. During the next few years he experienced every kind of temptation. He had to overcome desire and his inborn base nature, in order to maintain the stillness in his mind. Only then could he be a true master of life and free from pain. The love he found led him to leave his beloved new home to return to his old. He knew how wrong his people were but compassion prevented him from turning his back on them. If only he could teach them to find God; to commune; they could be spared life after life of despair and of separateness. It wouldn't be easy. He knew that. How could he, a man who had rejected the trappings of this material world, of no fixed abode and dressed in rags, proclaim that the powerful Jewish Church was fundamentally wrong in its beliefs? It seemed impossible but he knew that he was an instrument of God and trusted Him. He knew that God was saddened by the suffering His offspring experienced in their 'unknowing stage' of development. He knew that God was all powerful and would, if he allowed, use his body to teach Mankind how to find God. It became clear that, in order to teach, he would have to gain their attention.

The more Joshua communed with God, the more mysteries were revealed. He came to realize that all the physical world was an illusion – created through Mankind's subconscious beliefs. He realized that by changing his beliefs he could overcome what we know as 'the laws of physics'. He could cure people of dire sickness if he could make them believe enough. He could even walk on water and much more. Joshua didn't particularly wish to perform such acts. In fact they tempted him. He had spent so much time overcoming his ego, and now it took even more effort to not grow vain and pompous when he had crowds of adoring villagers around him. He knew that vanity and arrogance would obscure his perception of God and therefore lead him back to unhappiness. However, these stunts served their purpose. He gained the publicity he needed to do his real work – teaching people the way to find God within themselves.

Joshua had continued to use his nickname he had acquired during his travels. The Greek friends he met called him 'Jesus', a Greek version of 'Joshua'. It was unusual in Israel at that time and added to the air of mystery necessary for his publicity. Of course, those who knew Joshua when he was a boy scoffed at this and thought he was seeking publicity to feed his own egotistic vanity.

'Who does he think he is?' they said. 'A carpenter's boy telling us that he knows better than our most aged and well-read priests?'

They had about as much time for him as the average, well-heeled churchgoer in Britain today would have for a ragged, no-fixed-abode tramp. Jesus had his followers though, although rejected by the 'upright, decent citizens' of his time. His followers were the very poor, the universally despised tax-gatherers, the whores and other outcasts to whom he showed compassion and understanding. However, it wasn't long before an outraged society turned against him and demanded his execution. Thus the body of Jesus was destroyed, although his consciousness never could be. He became one with the universal consciousness known as God, which he had already experienced in life during the exercises of stilling the mind, and which he so fervently advocated.

Like the majority of those in the West, my first encounter with the name and teachings of Jesus was through Sunday School and attendance at church services (Church of England). The message I got was that Jesus was God born as a human. God was portrayed as a man who created the Universe but lived separate from it in an ethereal abode called 'Heaven'. Mankind was allowed to live life as best he could and when he died, he was judged by God. This resulted in him being banished to an abode of everlasting torture called 'Hell', or admitted to live with God in Heaven.

I was told that, as long as I obeyed the Ten Commandments, attended church services and said 'The Lord's Prayer' every day, I would be admitted to Heaven.

I now see this system of beliefs as being very similar to that of Judaism and very different from what Jesus actually taught. If the Jewish concept of religion had been correct, Jesus wouldn't have wasted his time trying to teach his fellow countrymen something different, particularly when he correctly predicted that it would result in outrage and his murder.

I hope to show the real message of Jesus which I feel has been lost from our present institutionalized religion. I also hope to show that Jesus was anti-institutionalized religion, and the fact that his name is associated with it at present is an enigma. I

14

shall be calling on sources outside the Bible. The four gospels together with the epistles of St Paul, had come to be accepted as reliable by about AD 130. The remaining books of the New Testament won gradual acceptance until by about the time of St Athanasius (c.369) the New Testament as we have it now was generally accepted as inspired scripture. I believe that the New Testament is an edited selection of the writings on him and his teachings; edited to make the message more acceptable to the established society of the time. Since then, other sources of information have been discovered, which were buried deliberately by the true followers of Christ. At this time they were persecuted, tortured and murdered for being 'heretics'. These Gnostics, as they were known, were groups of monks who came to know God in a literal sense, by communion with Him. By 'communion' I do not mean that they gathered in special buildings to receive bread and wine from a man dressed in special clothing, I mean actual comm-*union*; uniting with God and, in doing so, coming to know Him and His will. This I believe was what Jesus did and was murdered for, and is what he tried to teach us to do.

The other sources of information I use are from the fifty-two books dug up in 1945 by two peasants in the valley of the Upper Nile, Egypt, while they were seeking fertilizer for their fields. They are now called the Nag Hammadi Library. They were the treasures of a non-orthodox Christian monastery. A Roman garrison just across the river from the monastery housed an army that was used to liquidate by fire and sword non-orthodoxy. This was how orthodox christianity (which has become the present Catholic and Eastern Orthodox Churches) was adopted as the official religion of the Roman Empire. No doubt the monks could see what was coming to them and buried the books just in time.

In particular I shall be quoting from the Gospel of Thomas, written by the apostle Didymos Judas Thomas, popularly known as 'Doubting Thomas'. It is very different from the Gospels of the Bible in that it is a collection of sayings by Jesus called 'logia'. It doesn't record his life history as the Biblical gospels. The logia are at first difficult to interpret, having deep inner meanings of an esoteric, mystical nature. The same can be said about the teachings found in the writings of the Essenes.

The Essenes were a brotherhood, or sect, of men living in a

15

desert at the time of Christ and hundreds, if not thousands, of years prior to this. It is claimed that Jesus lived with them and became a Grand-master. (Remember that the Bible does not record Jesus' life between the approximate ages of thirteen and thirty years.) They lived in harmony with, and worshipped, nature. They saw God in everything. They prayed to their Mother Earth and their Heavenly Father, believing that the consciousness of mankind was a bridge between the two. Their life was simple and hard, rejecting materialism. Instead they sought spiritual treasures through a life of prayer and meditation.

Such teachings had no meaning for me until I experienced true meditation. Meditation is the act of stilling the mind completely through various natural techniques. When the mind is completely still, that is without any thought, yet fully alert and conscious, one undergoes an experience that defies description. It is an extinction of one's personality, or 'ego', and finding that what is left is a Universal Consciousness that is God. It is finding God within oneself; communion with the One . . . the All. Such an experience cannot ever be conveyed by words. One can only convey the experience by showing others how to find it themselves.

I now see that the teachings of Jesus, Buddha, Hindu and Taoist teachings, and probably teachings in all religions and philosophies have this common factor. In essence they all show how to live life unhindered by clinging thoughts of guilt, fear, doubt, and desires for worldly things. The only way the great teachers have ever been able to help their followers was by parables, logia. This must have been particularly true when teaching those of no formal education, such as in Jesus' time.

Their advice can be summarized by the phrase: 'Look where I have looked if you would see what I have seen'.

THE MYSTICAL CHRIST

The Christ I know and love was a human being; born with the same tendencies towards greed, avarice, lust, desires for prestige, fears, doubts and so forth, as ourselves. However, he overcame them to unite with God and showed us how to do likewise. He referred to himself as the 'son of man'. He often said that God and he were one. By the latter he meant that he had achieved oneness with God by stilling the mind; conquering the 'ego'. He did not consider himself as having potential that others could not achieve. He told us that if *we* have faith as small as a mustard seed, *we* can move mountains. (Note the '*we*', not 'I'.) Certainly he knew that God had put him on Earth for a special purpose and that he was destined to fulfil the prophecies in order to convince mankind that his way was *the* way. This does not, however, make him the God separate from Creation, that the Church would have us see. This whole concept of a separate, vengeful God, looking down on mankind, was what he set out to destroy. That was the Jewish concept perpetuated by the institutionalized religion of the time (and this time, in the Christian Church!).

Jesus was a rebel who set out to overthrow 'the establishment'. He was an anarchist who wanted to change the human condition, not through violence but by changing human consciousness – ending fear, doubt, and greed, and replacing them with love and trust in God. He knew that this would not be easy and wouldn't be achieved within his lifetime. However, he sowed the seed and it has grown slowly over the past two thousand years. Now, Mankind stands on the brink of a new age of wisdom and enlightenment. More and more people are believing in the possibility. More and more people are coming to know the God within themselves. However, there are still many who dismiss such concepts as preposterous. For them, the *real* world is one of aggression and greed. Peace for them is an armed truce. When such people exist as one's own family, neighbours, friends, it is easy to hide from one's beliefs and

17

accept their concept of the harsh 'reality'. It is easy to believe them when they call one a dreamer, or idealist who needs to see reality as it is; the way it's always been.

This is when such people become one's enemies, because they impose restrictions on one's beliefs.

I quote from my favourite rebel (Jesus, if you haven't guessed!):

> 'Do not think that I have come to bring peace on earth; I have not come to bring peace but a sword; for I have come to set a man against his father, and a daughter against her mother, and a daughter-in-law against her mother-in-law; and a man's foes will be those of his own household.'

THE IMPORTANCE
OF BELIEF

If one doesn't believe in God then, for you, God doesn't exist. If one doesn't believe in a heaven, then it is impossible to enter that state of consciousness. A sick person cannot become well unless he or she believes that it is possible. Jesus only cured those who had faith in his ability to cure. He asked them if they had faith before he cured them. Every doctor, herbalist, witch doctor or healer knows this. Drugs, herbs, and rituals are tools to increase a patient's faith. It must be said that drugs and herbs provide the building materials for the body to heal, but the process cannot occur without belief in that possibility.

Similarly, a witch doctor can kill by making his victim believe that the spell he has cast has that power. This is a problem in Western medicine at the moment. If a doctor tells the patient that he or she is dying of cancer, heart disease, AIDS, or whatever, that information is likely to shorten the patient's life. You can say that it is due to the stress produced by the diagnosis, but it amounts to the same thing.

There is no such thing as a lucky pessimist. If you spend your life believing that each day will bring misery and hardship, it inevitably does. Conversely, 'positive thinking', optimism, brings good fortune.

To the scientifically educated this seems to be nonsense. How can thoughts or beliefs affect anything solid and physical? If one learns about the new physics, since Einstein's brilliant work, and quantum mechanics, one gets a clue. The remarkable conclusion of physicists in this field is that what we perceive to be solid, actually isn't. Let me explain. Every schoolboy knows that matter is composed of minute particles called atoms. What wasn't known until recently is that atoms are actually composed of energy and space. The components of atoms are not solid; they are energy with relatively large spaces between the components in the centre and the electrons which encompass them. This means that the chair you are sitting on, your body, everything in the whole universe is actually energy and space.

What are thoughts composed of? Electrical energy passing through the cells (neurons) of the brain. These staggering concepts don't provide proof, but they certainly make my original statements more believable, i.e. that beliefs (energy) can affect physical matter (also energy).

For thousands of years mystics have told us that the world we live in is illusory. Could it be that the universe we live in is illusory? Could it be that we could change the universe by changing our beliefs? Is it possible that we could walk on water, cure by touch alone, levitate or move mountains, if we had faith as small as a mustard seed? It would seem so from Jesus' teachings.

Many believe in the widespread prophecies of a coming New Age of wisdom and enlightenment. However, not enough as yet. As long as the majority of mankind believes in a world of armed truces, inherent human aggression, greed and evil, that is the world we impose on ourselves. When the majority believe in the coming new age, it will happen.

Ken Carey talks about a remarkable theory in his book *Terra Christa*. He quotes a scientific observation of monkeys living on a group of islands. Every day these monkeys on one of the islands were fed by the scientists.

In time, the monkeys learned to wash the food left on the beach to remove the sand. As more and more learned this skill, a point was reached when suddenly all had learned the skill. The remarkable thing was that the skill was also shown on neighbouring islands, although there was no means for monkeys to travel between or communicate to their fellows. It was postulated that once sufficient numbers of the species had learnt the skill, a fundamental change occurred in the species group consciousness, so that all had the new skill.

Ken Carey postulates that the same may hold true of human beings, and that once sufficient numbers of us achieve 'God consciousness' (or 'enlightenment') a fundamental change will occur in the consciousness of our species. The New Age (or 'Aquarian Age') will have come upon us.

Ken Carey also postulates that the second coming of Christ will not be his coming as a physical man but his consciousness

20

within us. 'Christ consciousness', or 'God consciousness' is within us, slowly growing as more and more of us still our minds to find the God within.

If the human race could meditate at a specific time, say sunrise, each day, the enlightenment process would occur like a wave through our consciousness, going from East to West. Jesus told us his second coming would be 'as the lightning flashes and lights up the sky from one side to the other, so will the Son of Man be in his days'.

THE IMPORTANCE OF THOUGHTS

When I was a child, attending church services, I could never come to terms with the concept of 'sinning in thought, word and deed'. I could see how it was wrong to say bad things and even more so to do bad things, but I couldn't see how I could sin in thought. I believed that thoughts were beyond my control and therefore I couldn't be held responsible for them. I now know that I was wrong and that the concept of sinning by thought is under-explained by the Church.

Certainly, thoughts enter our head from the sub-conscious, without our wish and beyond our control. However, we have the choice between letting them pass on, or keeping them in our conscious mind. We can be guilty of entertaining bad thoughts.

What are bad thoughts? Thoughts which feed the ego; desires that keep the ego alive, obscuring our perception of God and knowledge of our Universal Self, which is a part of God. I'm talking about the deadly sins which we're all guilty of at some time or other: greed, avarice, lust, jealousy, arrogant thoughts of self-importance and vanity, fears born out of not trusting God.

Many people are smug in their self righteousness if they manage to live life without breaking the Ten Commandments. They think it is a great achievement if they manage not to commit adultery, steal, murder and so forth. However, Jesus tells us that if we entertain desires to do such things, it is as bad as actually doing them. I quote:

> 'You have heard that it was said "you shall not commit adultery". But I tell you that everyone who looks at a woman lustfully has already committed adultery with her in his heart.'

These thoughts I have called 'sticky thoughts', because they come into our consciousness and stick there; feeding our ego,

22

obscuring our perception of the God within. It is God's will that they do enter our minds. This is how He tests us. By overcoming such thoughts we gain merit; progress in our spiritual evolution. By allowing the thoughts to stay, the resultant distancing from God brings dis-ease; lack of ease, or inner peace, that manifests itself in physical and/or mental illness.

The process of gaining control over thoughts, and ultimately stilling the mind completely, is called meditation. This practice is an essential part, if not the central part, of Eastern religions and philosophies, as it indeed was in Celtic Christian practice. I believe it is the essence of Christ's teaching, although now obscured by two thousand years of dogma. All sin by word and deed originate from sinful thought. The people he tried to teach thought that they could find God and Heaven by obeying certain commands concerning their words and deeds alone. This was born out of their misconception of the nature of God and Heaven. They saw God as separate from man, looking down from a separate Heaven, judging their words and deed. They failed to see that God was within and that Heaven was uniting with God, by suppression of the ego.

Imagine a pond with a rippled surface. You cannot see within unless the pond calms, and then you can see below. This is the Eastern analogy of the mind: the ripples are the thoughts and desires which comprise one's ego or personality. Once they are calmed by meditation one sees the true self; the Universal self. One identifies with, becomes one with, God. This is the act of communion with God that Jesus taught. He instructed us to consume him, flesh and blood: 'He who eats my flesh and drinks my blood abides in me, and I in him.'

He was aware that many of his followers thought they could achieve Heaven by obeying his commands concerning way of life. He was saying that it is not enough. We have to achieve the God consciousness that he had. Then, and only then, would he be abiding in us and us in him. The bread and wine are symbols of our taking him and his consciousness into ourselves.

The church service of Holy Communion is a useful reminder of this, but in my experience, the inner esoteric meaning behind the ritual is not fully explained.

I do not believe it is essential to attend such rituals, but I do know that it is essential to commune with God by stilling the mind in meditation, for spiritual evolution to occur.

I now present an information sheet, I wrote to give my patients, whom I was trying to help, in the psychiatric service:

'Making the Two One'

An essay on meditation, a natural way to calm a troubled mind by Dr Henry Whitehead.

In recent years scientists have shown us that human consciousness, what we experience as 'life', is made up of two types blended together. The brain is made up of two halves, left and right. Each half seems to be involved with different, to some extent opposite, types of thinking. The left brain, which is the most active in most people, is involved with the logical thinking we need to survive in daily life. It deals with solving problems, categorizing things, analysing and also forming words in thought and speech.

The right brain, however, is involved with forming mental images; appreciating beauty and music; the sense of rhythm; abstract concepts, e.g. love.

These two opposites could almost be described as masculine and feminine, although they have nothing to do with sex.

The left side is more active than the right, particularly in people who don't work in creative jobs or live in beautiful surroundings. However, when scientists studied the 'brainwaves' (electrical activity of the brain) of people who meditate, they found that this imbalance corrected itself. The two sides became balanced and in harmony. It was then clear that meditation was far from just Eastern mumbo-jumbo with no relevance to us in the West. It is a very real experience – a different form of consciousness. The techniques of meditation are all aimed at increasing the activity of the right brain, decreasing the activity of the left brain, or both. This corrects the imbalance and produces stilling of the mind. In fact true meditation begins when thoughts stop altogether. However, it may take years of practice before this happens, and although this is the goal, it doesn't mean that we don't experience benefit right from the start. It does mean that the feeling of calm and peace becomes better with practice.

Mental illness often starts with our thoughts going out of control. We have all experienced the sensation of our minds 'buzzing' with thoughts as we scurry around trying to do half a dozen things at once. When those thoughts become dominated with worries; such as fears for the future, we are on the way to mental illness unless something is done. Unfortunately, some people quiet their minds with drugs or alcohol. By doing this, the worry is not overcome, but pushed deeper inside us to be faced at a later date. Thus if drugs or alcohol are abused for this, a kind of large 'bank' of fears and worries builds up, to be overcome in future. The bigger it is, the more difficult to overcome, and even when it is overcome (usually with psychiatric help), each day brings new worries and fears. However, if we confront these daily and learn to still our minds naturally, we stay on top of things and grow stronger. The benefits of meditation don't stop with helping our mental health. Regular meditation helps keep one's blood pressure low and makes us less prone to heart attacks. It also keeps a substance in the blood called cortisone low. This natural steroid is produced in excess when we are stressed and has the unfortunate effect of weakening the bodies defence system (immune system) against infection and cancer. Thus meditation makes us less likely to have these and more able to fight them even if we do.

MEDITATION TECHNIQUES

There are many described, but broadly speaking they fall into two kinds:

1. 'MINDFULNESS'

This is a Buddhist term and describes a state of mind where one is totally aware of all one is aware. For instance, while reading this you are not aware of your breathing; the sound of traffic or wind outside; the feel of the chair in contact with your body; until they are mentioned. In this technique we *do* become aware of all sensations and in doing so, the mind becomes still to word thoughts and worries.

First sit comfortable and upright with your hands together and legs crossed. It doesn't matter if this is on a cushion or seated on a chair, as long as you are comfortable. You must be upright otherwise you will tend to become drowsy and drift off to sleep. The hands and legs are together to help you feel them, and become aware of their presence. Loosen your clothing or anything which is restricting.

Now close your eyes and become aware of your breathing. Try to let it become slower, deeper and silent. Become aware of its rhythm (a right brain activity).

Now start to build a mental image of yourself occupying the space where you are sitting. Picture your eyes first; next picture your hands and then your feet. As you do this you will become aware of how they feel and relax the muscles in them. Next, join these images with each other as you build an image of your whole self. Try to imagine a point in the centre of your chest, by your heart, is projecting a hologram image of light of you. As the image forms you should become aware of all parts of your body at once. Next feel warmth and love radiate from that point alongside the light. Once your body image is filled, let it shine out to fill the room you are in and then on out in all directions to fill the universe.

Next become aware of all the sounds around you. Do *not* try to identify them, (categorizing is a left brain function). Simply become aware. If any thoughts drift into your mind let them pass out again without sticking.

Practise this at least twice a day each day at *regular* times and also in between when you become aware that your mind is starting to 'buzz' with thoughts and worries. Try to do it for at least five to ten minutes and aim to extend it to twenty to thirty minutes as you get better.

HOW DOES IT WORK? The mental image you formed was right brain activity. So was the awareness of the rhythm of your breathing. So was the awareness of yourself as a whole. So was dealing with the abstract concept of love.

The right brain became more active and left brain less so. The imbalance was corrected. The two became one.

Some people like to meditate whilst listening to relaxing music, the appreciation of which is another right brain activity. Although this can be helpful at first, and very relaxing, if one is aiming for complete stilling of the mind, it is better to be in silence, or amidst quiet natural sounds of the countryside or sea.

2. CONCENTRATIVE TECHNIQUES:

Instead of becoming aware of all sensations, it is possible to drive out thought and worry by concentrating very hard on one. For instance one might gaze continuously at one object and try to 'become one with it' – excluding all other sensations and thoughts. The object may be some revered symbol of religion or may equally be a tree, flower, vase, sunset, jewel or anything else.

Alternatively, one might concentrate on rhythm and chant something repetitively. This may be a prayer e.g. the use of rosary beads in Catholic Christian prayer, or it could also be some 'positive affirmation'. The latter is the same as 'positive thinking', but said aloud. For instance one could repetitively chant 'I – am – strong – today; I – am – strong – today – . . . ' – the disadvantage of this method is that if the chant is too repetitive it might make you drowsy and fall into a trance or stupor. Thus it is best to change the wording or pitch of what you say, now and again.

Personally I find 'mindfulness' the best technique to start with.

DIFFICULTIES: 'STICKY THOUGHTS'

A characteristic of the human mind is that we have difficulty focussing our attention on any one thing for any reasonable length of time. Instead our minds flit from one thing to another – all kinds of jumbled thoughts, interspersed with snatches of pop tunes, T.V. jingles and so forth. Buddhists describe this as the 'monkey mind'. It resembles a monkey swinging from branch to branch of a tree, unable to settle on one. Meditation trains one to develop the ability to fix one's attention, but clearly this takes considerable practice.

As one become an observer of one's own thoughts, insight develops into the cause of one's problems. It becomes obvious that certain thoughts are more difficult to dispel from one's mind than others. Thus we can identify what it is that prevents us finding peace in meditation. Examples of particularly 'sticky' thoughts are: guilt, hatred towards someone, (including yourself), lust, envy, fears of the future (e.g. financial problems, health, death), avarice, worrying about how other people see us, and so forth. Resolving that problem is, of course, another matter. However, experienced meditators often say that since starting the practice, they can view their lives from a new perspective. Their values may change; something that once was all important may become insignificant and vice versa.

LIFESTYLE

The more we can become aware of our body, the easier it is for 'mindfulness' meditations. Yoga exercises, or Tai Chi (another Eastern exercise system), are designed to stretch every part of the body and in doing so, increases our awareness of it.

Obviously, a lifestyle that promotes self-respect and prevents guilt is necessary. Also, we need to resolve any bitterness or guilt from our past.

Living in an environment of natural beauty, away from noise is ideal. However, if this is not possible, a daily walk in a park is beneficial. Taking up creative hobbies is another way of stimulating the right brain. This is why painting, pottery, writing and so forth are so relaxing.

Before the advent of television, people would read books. This makes one form mental images (right brain activity) and is more relaxing than watching television, where the image is formed for you.

Religion or philosophy often helps people cope with fear of the future and death.

RELIGION AND MEDITATION

You do not have to be religious to benefit from meditation. The majority of people in the West who meditate, do so purely as an aid to relaxation and mental health. However, it is well known that meditation is essential religious practice for Buddhists, Hindus and other religions. Many Christians say to me that they would like to meditate, but fear that it might be against their religion. Obviously, if meditating promotes a feeling of guilt it will be counter-productive, and a perfect stilling of the mind would be impossible.

Meditation is associated with religion because of the experienced meditator's description of a perfectly still mind. This largely indescribable experience has been described as 'heaven', 'ecstasy', 'unity with God' and so forth. If such an experience sounds frightening, be reassured that it could never occur unless you wished it to, and relaxed completely, as a small babe-in-arms!

To my fellow Christians I proffer the following extract from *The Gospel of Thomas* by Didymos Judas Thomas, (the disciple who became known as 'Doubting Thomas' (discovered in Egypt in 1945)):

> Jesus saw children who were being suckled. He said to his disciples: These children who are being suckled are like those who enter the Kingdom. They said to him: Shall we then, being children, enter the Kingdom? Jesus said to them: When you make the two One, and you make the inner even as the outer, and the outer even as the inner, and the above even as the below, so that you will make the male and the female into a single One, in order that the male is not made male, nor the female made female; when you make eyes in place of an eye, and a hand in place of a hand, and a foot in place of a foot, and an image in place of an image, then shall you enter the Kingdom.

I have tried to explain the brain mechanisms of physiology of meditation because I feel that Western people of this generation will not accept anything that they cannot grasp through logical (left-brained) rationalization. This is the result of our scientific biased education. I am not trying to reduce God or heaven to a chemical process in the brain. The fact that certain changes are observable in the brain when one enters God consciousness does not diminish the importance of the experience. Remember that the brain, like all physical matter, is not what it seems.

My interpretation of the preceding logia from the Gospel of Thomas is that it is a meditation technique involving formation of a mental image of oneself. In doing this the two aspects of consciousness become balanced and then a change occurs so that neither aspect of consciousness is as before. 'The male is not made made, nor the female made female'. The conscious-

29

ness one enters is indescribable. However, it is the consciousness we all knew as a suckling baby, but have forgotten. It is a purity of consciousness that is pure love without thought, fear, worry or perception of time. As one becomes one with all that there is, i.e. God, there is no above or below; no inner or outer, just love and oneness. There is no boredom or desire for anything. As the ego dies, if only for a second, (which could equally be an eternity during the experience), there is loss of the individual self. What is left is God consciousness – Heaven. Many people think that their personality persists after death and that they drift around as a disembodied spirit identical to their living selves. But which personality? One's personality changes continuously throughout life. Who is the same person when aged forty years as he or she was when a teenager, or child, or old person? People with advanced dementia or schizophrenia often have no perceptible personality. This disturbs society so much that they are locked away from it. It feeds Mankind's greatest fear that perhaps after death there is nothing; extinction. From the ego's point of view, this is true. Death of the ego occurs with death of the brain. How bearable this is depends on how well we have prepared for the experience. Meditation is preparation for the dying experience; preparation for meeting and uniting with the Oneness that is God. Without preparation, the experience is the terror of Hell. Even if the death of the brain occurs in milliseconds to an outside observer, such as through death by explosion, to the one experiencing it, it would last an eternity of terror.

However, if one daily communes with God; practising release of the ego, learning to trust Him as we did when small babies, there is no fear.

Many who have had near death experiences talk about a remembrance of their whole lives occurring in an instant. 'My whole life flashed before my eyes' is a common phrase. While one is experiencing guilt and self-hate one cannot experience unity with God. We will each judge ourselves during the death experience. The same is true during meditation. One's mind cannot settle while there is guilt, or resentment or fear, jealousy, or lust. However, by daily meditation we learn to release these negative feelings. One comes to believe Christ's statement that there is no sin so great that God won't forgive – if we believe it to be so, and truly repent.

SEEING THE LIGHT

I have described the experience of overwhelming love and Oneness one finds when the mind (or ego) is stilled. I have tried to explain the lack of perception of time, which only occurs when there is stream of thought. There is another quality to the experience; that of wondrous light.

This light is, again, beyond description, but suffice it to say that the brilliance is unsurpassed, yet never dazzling or uncomfortable.

I quote from Jesus from the Gospel of Thomas (logia 24):

His disciples said: Show us the place where you are,
because it is necessary for us to seek after it. He said
to them: He who has ears let him hear; there is light
at the centre of a man of light and he illumines the
whole world. If he does not shine, there is darkness.

This is my reason for imagining myself glowing with light and love during meditation. We must all glow with this 'lovelight', as much as we can. With practice it is possible in every situation, not just whilst sitting or kneeling with eyes closed.

Love is the most healing force in the Universe. It is an antidote for all fear, doubt, hatred, jealously, guilt, lust, greed and so forth.

Do not think that you have to have a partner to feel love. True, unconditional love can be felt without any one specific object. One must love all creation, because all creation is God.

31

A DISTURBING EXPERIENCE

I quote from the Gospel of Thomas, logia 2:

> Jesus said: Let him who seeks not cease from seeking
> until he finds; and when he finds, he will be dis-
> turbed; and when he is disturbed, he will marvel,
> and he shall reign over the All.

The first time one unites with God it is a disturbing experience. To find a cessation of thoughts, memories, personality, revealing the magnificent oneness of God, the All, turns one around. One finds that all preconceived notions concerning self and existence are destroyed at a single stroke.

After my first experience I was afraid and yet awe-struck at the same time. I could not help but try and analyse the experience in scientific medical terms. Had I gone mad? Did I have some epileptic phenomenon?

Deep inside I knew that somehow I had 'met God' and that He had spoken to me, but not with booming words; rather He had revealed Himself to me. However, I still could not believe. Things like that surely didn't happen to ordinary people like me, in these times. They may happen to great prophets like Moses, but to me? In twentieth century England?

I tried to ignore and forget the experience but I could not. I knew I was hiding from God. I knew God wanted me to commune; wants all of us to commune, so that His love can guide us.

That was four years ago. I have tried to commune every day since. However, I must confess that sometimes I have allowed worldly affairs to distract me.

Satan is always trying to lead one away from this experience by titillating the ego with worldly things; making excuses for one.

Do not consider Satan to be a mythological creature with horns and tail. He is within us all; the evil aspect of human consciousness, but, like God, an entity in His own right, with his own collective evil consciousness. Believe me, Satan's greatest trick is to make one not believe in his existence.

In order to emphasize the need to fight Satan's excuses he sends us, trying to keep our consciousness bound into this world, I quote Jesus' parable:

A man once gave a great banquet, and invited many; and at the time for the banquet he sent his servant to say to those who had been invited, 'Come, for all is now ready.' But they all alike began to make excuses. The first said to him, 'I have bought a field, and I must go out and see it; I pray you, have me excused.' And another said, 'I have bought five yoke of oxen, and I go to examine them; I pray you, have me excused.' And another said, 'I have married a wife, and therefore I cannot come.' So the servant came and reported this to his master.

Then the householder in anger said to his servant, 'Go out quickly to the streets and lanes of the city, and bring in the poor and the maimed, and blind and lame.' And the servant said, 'Sir, what you commanded has been done, and still there is room.' And the master said to the servant, 'Go out to the highways and hedges, and compel people to come in, that my house may be filled. For I tell you, none of those men who were invited shall taste my banquet.'

In this parable, the master is God, the servant is Christ; the banquet is the Kingdom of Heaven and we are the invited people.

The more one communes with God the easier and more wondrous the experience becomes. In time it is not disturbing; just marvellous. Our whole life must be dedicated to becoming comfortable in unity with God. This is the importance of stilling the mind and finding God within. I must point out that this does not necessarily have to be by the practice of oriental techniques. Many people have found God without knowingly meditating in the formal sense. God may reveal Himself during the rapture of gazing on His created beauty, during a walk in the country, or in listening to music, for instance. However, God is only revealed when the mind is stilled from worldly desires, anxieties, anger, arrogance.

EXPANSION
OF CONSCIOUSNESS

In Buddhist philosophy the lotus flower is a sacred analogy of the experience of expansion of consciousness on uniting with God. As the lotus flower grows, it starts in mud, grows up through relatively clear water and on reaching the light at the pond's surface, bursts into a beautiful, expansive bloom. This represents man's consciousness, starting in the mud of worldliness, reaching towards Heaven, and on finding the 'lovelight' of God, expanding into unity with Him.

Jesus had a similar analogy. I quote from the Gospel of Thomas, logia 20:

> The Disciples said to Jesus: Tell us, what is the kingdom of heaven like? He said to them: It is like a grain of mustard, smaller than all seeds; but when it falls on the tilled earth, it sends forth a large stem and becomes a shelter for the birds of the sky.

The grain of mustard is man's consciousness. The fact that it must fall on the tilled earth to grow, points out the need to 'work' for its growth, by leading a spiritual life. The end product is an expanding collective consciousness such as a large tree with birds in its branches.

HOLY SPIRIT GUIDED INTUITION

Intuition is a difficult thing to describe, but most of us know it. It is another function of the right cerebral hemisphere of the brain. It is the sudden inspiration or knowing that we get without having thought things through in the usual logical, left brained way. We suddenly know something is right, or something is wrong, although we can't say why. Traditional, scientific method scorns such knowledge although many of our greatest geniuses and inventors have had such inspirations. Usually though, they don't reveal their inspiration until they have verified it through scientific deduction. This 'other way' of obtaining knowledge is intuition.

Such knowledge comes from the collective consciousness which is usually sub-conscious. We do not receive intuition, inspirational insights, while the conscious mind is 'buzzing' with its usual thoughts. Access to the collective consciousness within, which is God, comes by stilling the mind.

The insights it, or He provides can guide and comfort us. God shows us His will by this. It is what is called 'The Holy Spirit', or as Jesus called it 'the Counsellor'.

Before the days of scientific medicine, the healer would enter a meditative state and 'dowse' for healing herbs. He or she would ask God for His guidance and walk through the forests, or by the hedgerows, looking for herbs which 'felt right'. Animals also possess this gift. Sick dogs chew on 'Couch-grass', or 'Dog-grass' as it is sometimes called. It is now known to contain natural anti-biotic substances, but the dog didn't have to analyse it in a laboratory to know this!

The Holy Spirit can guide in all things once we have attuned to Him, and learned to trust Him. The Holy Spirit is the God within. I quote from the Gospel of Thomas, logia 6:

'His disciples questioned, they said to him: Do you wish that we should fast? And in which way should we pray? Should we give alms? And what diet should be observe? Jesus said: Do not lie, and do not do what you dislike, for all things are revealed before the heaven. For there is nothing hidden that shall not be manifest, and there is nothing concealed that shall remain without being revealed.'

I think that there is something lost in translation here. At first it appears that Jesus was saying 'do what you want'. However, I think the correct translation is 'do what feels right', i.e. let the Holy Spirit guide your intuition instead of blindly following man-made rules. Note that he says 'all things are revealed before the heaven'. It is in the meditative state prior to entering into unity with God, or coming away from it, that esoteric knowledge is given by God. This is quite different from doing whatever feels good through gratifying the ego's desires. The Holy Spirit also gives us the words to teach others, if we ask and believe. I quote Jesus from the Gospel of Mark:

'Behold, I send you out as sheep in the midst of wolves: so be wise as serpents and innocent as doves. Beware of men; for they will deliver you up to councils, and flog you in their synagogues, and you will be dragged before governors and kings for my sake to bear testimony before them and the Gentiles. When they deliver you up, do not be anxious how or what you shall speak; for what you shall say will be given to you in that hour. For it is not you who speak, but the Spirit of your Father speaking through you.'

There is a great tendency in institutionalized religion, and human society in general, for a multitude of rules and regulations to be made. Jesus teaches us to not live by these but by God inspired intuition. When he was reprimanded by the priests for breaking the rule concerning not working on the Sabbath, by healing, he said this (Extract from Gospel of John):

'Moses gave you circumcision (not that it is from Moses, but from the fathers), and you circumcise a man upon the Sabbath. If on the Sabbath a man received circumcision, so that the law of Moses may not be broken, are you angry with me because on the Sabbath I made a man's whole body well? Do not

36

judge by appearances, but judge with right judgement.'

To live solely by left-brain rational thinking and reject God's gift of inspirational insight is to blaspheme against the Holy Spirit. As Jesus says:

'Therefore I tell you, every sin and blasphemy will be forgiven men, but the blasphemy against the Holy Spirit will not be forgiven. And whoever says a word against the Son of Man will be forgiven; but whoever speaks against the Holy Spirit will not be forgiven, either in this age or in the age to come.'

THE NATURE OF GOD

Christ rarely referred to God as 'God'. Instead he used terms such as 'the Father', 'our Father', 'my Father', 'the One' and 'the All'. He also said 'My Father and I are one' and 'My Father is greater than I'. I have said that God is the oneness of everything, to be true to my experience of Him. This so called 'pantheistic' concept is not recognized by the church. However, Christ said such things as:

> 'If you become my disciples and hear my logia, these stones will minister to you.'
>
> (Gospel of Thomas, logia 19)

and Jesus said:

> 'I am the light that is above them all. I am the All. The All comes forth from me, and the All reaches towards me. Cleave the wood, I am there; lift up the stone, and you shall find me there.'
>
> (Gospel of Thomas, logia 77)

Returning to the new physics we find truth in the proclamation of mystics of all religions and philosophies, namely, 'All is one.' We now know that space itself curves around the Black Holes that occur in it. Space is somethingness. This means that everything, absolutely everything, is connected. There is unity; a Oneness of everything to which we belong.

Christ's insistence that God is our 'Father' shows many characteristics of God. First, He is an entity with consciousness, who must be turned to and prayed to. Secondly, like earthly fathers, He loves us and wants us to be with Him. Thirdly, like earthly fathers, He punishes, by causing ill fortune to fall on us. However, this punishment is out of love not anger or hatred. Ill fortune occurs for a reason, the same as a good earthly father punishes a naughty child to change his or her behaviour. When we were children we could not understand how father or mother could spank us and yet tell us that they loved us, and that it was 'for our own good'. Similarly we don't understand why the tragedies of this life occur. When we were children we could not conceive of being different from that state; being an adult. Similarly, we cannot conceive of consciousness in the next world, in unity with God (until we commune with Him). Tragedy has to occur in this life. How else could we learn the necessary courage and trust in God, to evolve into the next life? It is easy to say we trust in God, but we can only be sure we do when that trust is tested, and we pass the test.

Mostly we want to grab a piece of 'the good times', nail it down, stand on it and resist change. That is because we don't know the wonder and glory of Heaven. This life is nothing in comparison, and the tragedies of it will soon be forgotten. We must never resist change. Life is a flowing event, from cradle to grave and beyond. This life can be compared to the nine months spent in the womb. It is preparation for the next life; nothing more, nothing less.

THE PURPOSE OF LIFE ON THIS EARTH

Many people are searching for a meaning to life. You don't have to go high in the Himalayas, or anywhere, to find it. All the answers are within ourselves. We are here to overcome our base, animalistic nature and to learn to love and trust God. It is simply that. It is impossible to unite with Him and know that indescribable joy unless we do.

Overcoming our fears, hatred and base nature is a formidable task, yet within the capability of everyone, whether young or old, intelligent or mentally handicapped. It could be compared with slaying a giant, and is by Jesus in the Gospel of Thomas, logia 98:

> 'Jesus said: The Kingdom of the Father is like a man who wishes to kill a giant. He drew the sword in his house, he stuck it through the wall in order to be assured that his hand would be confident. Then he slew the giant.'

This logia shows the need to practise overcoming our fear, hatred and base nature before death; to make sure we are confident we can do this on our deathbed. It shows the need to overcome those 'sticky thoughts' by stilling our minds in meditation.

THE RELATIONSHIP BETWEEN GOD CONSCIOUSNESS AND HUMAN CONSCIOUSNESS

I like Ken Carey's analogy of a hologram. If one takes one of these three-dimensional images and smashes it, one can pick up any piece and see the whole image in that piece. Such is the relationship between God consciousness and human consciousness. God is the whole hologram; we are the pieces. We are part of God, and yet the whole of God is within us.

A POLICY OF NOT CLINGING

I have talked about the need to not cling to thoughts; to allow them to come and go without settling to disturb one's peace. The same is true with the outside world. We all have a tendency to cling to things, to people, to places. Such clinging slows the progress of the soul's evolution. Christ's teachings against materialism are well known, though perhaps few understand why. It is not a rule to be followed blindly, as are any of his teachings. It is no good to live in poverty whilst still craving material things. One must choose to not cling. The more possessions one clings to the more difficult it is to leave them when one's time has come. The more one owns, the more one worries about breakage, theft and so on. The insurance companies capitalize on this fear, as they do on our fear for the future concerning health and death.

Owning things is not wrong as such, but clinging to them is, because it grounds the soul. When you find yourself thinking twice about lending something, or resisting an inner urge to travel because of the weight of your possessions, beware.

If you have an inner urge to travel; obey it. Many people cling to a piece of ground they call their own. How can we own the earth? It was created for all of us and belongs to all of us. Such clinging is born out of fear for the future; desire for the security of our old age. Fight your fears and learn to trust God. If you have an inner urge to travel it is the Holy Spirit leading you to new experiences; new temptations and fears to overcome; things to learn and things to teach. There is always work for God's children, although not always by contract to a business. Meeting people and learning or teaching spiritual matters is God's work. It is not God's will to travel purely for self gratification though. I have met many rich people whose life is devoted to being on beaches and taking from the world instead of giving. They are some of the most unhappy people I know. Life has no meaning for them. You cannot find paradise by simply finding a beautiful tropical island.

Clinging to people is also born out of fear for the future; insecurity due to not trusting God. It is God's will that we love Him above all that is on earth. If our peace depends on the presence of other people, we will be devastated when they leave or die.

It is Christ's specific instruction that we should love one another, including our enemies. There can be no inner peace unless it is so.

I quote Jesus in the Gospel of Thomas, logia 55:

'Jesus said: He who does not dislike his father and mother will not be able to become my disciple, and he who does not dislike his brothers and sisters and does not carry his cross in my way, will not be worthy of me.'

and from logia 101:

'He who does not dislike his father and his mother in my way will not be able to become my disciple; and he who does not love his Father and his Mother in my way will not be able to become my disciple for my mother has begotten me but my true Mother gave me life.'

At first these logia seem startling. What does Jesus mean by disliking our father and mother, brothers and sisters? It seems to contradict his instructions to love one another. What he means though, is that we must detach ourselves spiritually from all others, and love our true Mother, the Earth, and our Heavenly Father above all. How could the Christian religion have come about if Jesus and his disciples stayed at home, clinging to their mothers' apron strings? Of course, we must love and respect our parents, brothers and sisters and everybody but not above our love for God.

I quote from the Gospel of Thomas, logia 49:

'Jesus said: Happy are the "loners" and the chosen, for you shall find the Kingdom. Because you are from the heart of it, you shall go there again.'

and from logia 75:

'Jesus said: There are many standing at the door, but the "loners" are they who shall enter the marriage place.'

Being a 'loner' does not mean that we should all become hermits. It is God's will that we interact and love one another.

43

However, it does mean that we should not depend on anyone other than God for our peace. We should not cling to anyone lest it be God's will that they are taken from us.

There are times in our life when we must experience loneliness. Those who do, and conquer it, are those who turn inwards to find God. This is why it is God's will that we sometimes have our loved ones taken from us.

As a young man I was a 'people-pleaser'. I could not bear to be unpopular. I needed my gang of friends around me to be happy, living from one party to the next. Often I would compromise my ideals in order to be popular. The 'party crowd' shuns anyone who speaks of God. Let me assure you that there can never be true inner peace until one detaches from all that is in this world and turns inwards to God. I like the Sufi teaching of 'being in this world, but not of it'.

SEXUAL RELATIONSHIPS AND SEXUALITY

Sex is a gift from God, which like all His gifts, can be used or abused. When used according to God's will the sexual act is an expression of deep love. It can be a spiritual experience where there is love and no guilt. Such an experience can literally elevate one's consciousness to God. On the other hand, we find the pure animalistic lust expressed in acts such as sodomy, bestiality and the various other acts I find difficult to mention. Lust titillates the ego. Love helps one overcome the ego to find God within. In such an act of love, one is giving to one's partner and is more concerned with pleasing him or her than oneself. In an act of lust one is taking from the partner; using them to achieve self-gratification without any real thought for the partner.

Everybody experiences lust at some time. Like other aspects of our base nature, it is to be overcome. It is a 'sticky' thought that takes away our peace and prevents perception of God.

Adolescence is a particularly difficult time in this respect and masturbation is almost inevitable. However, this too can be done with love or lust in one's heart, depending on the fantasy one is entertaining in one's mind. Lust always promotes guilt and loss of self-respect. One must at least abstain from the pornography designed to promote lust.

The sexual act is also given to us for procreation. God wishes to use us to create new life and continue the miracle He started. The present evil Western society has practically stopped this process. People are encouraged to get into massive debts in order to possess material things, and then find that they 'can't afford' to have children. Many, however, use this as an excuse, because they prefer their electronic gadgetry to children.

Their logical left-brains come up with the excuse 'there's too many people in this world. There's not enough food to go around'. We all know deep inside that this isn't true. If the food and other wealth that our Mother Earth gives us was fairly distributed, there would be plenty to go around for everybody. Consider the money and human effort that is spent on armaments and maintaining our armed truce, the world leaders laughably call 'peace'. How much could be done to help Third World countries feed themselves! How much could be done to avoid out man-made ecological disasters!

THE MURDER OF
INNOCENTS

I gather that approximately 170,000 human babies are murdered each year in Britain alone, with the blessing of our authorities. 'Termination' is a euphemism for abortion. 'Abortion' is a euphemism for murder of babies. Again our logical left brain provides all kinds of excuses. 'I'm not ready to have a baby. It wouldn't be cared for properly.' 'The baby is deformed, it wouldn't be happy.' Deep down, our intuition knows that the murder of any baby is against God's will.

Fifty years ago the Nazis rationalized that the execution of the Jewish race was for the benefit of mankind by creating an Aryan super-race. Beware of left-brain rationalization.

If we are really worried about there being too many people on Earth it would be better to allow adults to die when their time has come instead of keeping people artificially alive with drugs and gadgetry. However, I *know* that God is in control and that the human population will self-regulate through natural God-given disasters.

If it is God's will that a baby dies, he or she will do by His hand in the form of disease or other disaster. It is not God's will that we are instrumental in taking human life. We must love and nourish as best we can and trust in God that that baby is on earth for a purpose, even though it may die by God's hand at an early age.

THE CONCEPT OF REINCARNATION

Many Eastern religions and philosophies believe that one may take more than one life on Earth before finally uniting with God in Heaven. I cannot understand why the Christian Church finds this concept contrary to Christ's teachings. If God is merciful enough to give us another chance to learn love and trust in Him, this only shows His great love for us. Perhaps this 'other chance' may involve only a short life on Earth, and this would explain the otherwise seemingly senseless death of children.

The soul of an unrepented sinner might choose to be reincarnated into a difficult life, as a cripple for instance, on facing God at death. He or she might choose to undertake such a task to prove to God that they are worthy of uniting with Him, by overcoming such adversity.

Christ tells us the John the Baptist was Elijah come again. (see Matthew 11, 10-14; Matthew 17, 10-13.) Some souls, although worthy of entering Heaven, might choose to offput their personal Heaven to re-incarnate and help their spiritual brothers and sisters on Earth find God.

Christ said: 'Before Abraham was, I was.' Such a concept is known to all believers of re-incarnation. We have all existed since the beginning of time, as part of God. We are from God and we are on the path to returning to Him.

Christ did not make this a major part of his teaching, however, because it is not important for us to know. Also, the utter outrage he would have received from society would have made them turn away from him without listening further to the essential teachings he had to offer.

It is not God's will that we remember our past lives, if any, because the memory of so much tragedy and tribulation would be more than we could bear. Many people try, and perhaps succeed, in gaining these memories by certain techniques. If the motive for this is curiosity or trying to gain proof of life after death, this is wrong. Instead we should trust God and believe that if He thinks it is necessary for us to know, He will let us know.

THE NEED FOR PRAYER

Communion with God should result in a two-way communication between God and man. I have spoken about how God's Holy Spirit can 'speak' to one; not so much as a big booming voice from above or within, but by a giving of inspirations and insights. One must also talk to God, either outwardly or inwardly. God only exists as a distinct conscious entity, for you, if you believe He does.

If you believe He is a conscious entity within, you will want to thank Him for His gifts, ask Him for guidance, beg forgiveness for yourself and others.

Prayer should not consist of reciting words written by others. One must approach God by stilling the mind and open your heart to Him. Tell Him of your troubles. Thank Him for them; for the tests He sends us are for our own good, and will result in greater strength and trust in Him, once they have been overcome.

Be careful what you pray for. Let your requests be motivated by love, not greed. This is particularly when praying for the acquisition of a material object. Mainly we should be praying for world enlightenment; a growing of God consciousness throughout our race. Also, we should be praying for understanding; insights into how we can help ourselves, i.e. knowledge of God's will.

There is great virtue in praying for others more than yourself. If you wish someone to be healed, whilst meditating one can imagine the loved one's image in place of your image. Then feel the lovelight glow to fill up that image. Do this also with the images of your enemies, so that they too will find God and make peace with you.

Imagine the whole Earth glowing with lovelight and *believe* in the growing God consciousness within us all.

A CONCEPT OF DEMONS

Many times I have told people that I do not believe in distinct disembodied evil entities that can leap on one and make one evil against one's will. I believed that evil is something within man's consciousness only. This put me at odd's with Christ's mention of demons and unclean spirits, which He cast out from people in order to heal them.

I suppose my medical concepts of neuroanatomy and physiology made me vain enough to believe I knew better. I saw the concept of demons as being archaic and born out of ignorance.

I still believe that evil is something rooted in all human consciousness and is to be overcome. However, it has been revealed to me today that the process of conceiving that fears, doubts, lust, greed, etc., are demons attacking one, is a useful tool in ridding oneself of them. What one truly believes to be true becomes true. By believing that one's 'sticky thoughts' are demons within, one can embody them and cast them out.

Imagine that love is a positive energy and that the demons are negative. By glowing with lovelight, imagine the demons being expelled from your soul.

Satan would have you believe that his demons are not demons, but a part of your consciousness that you can do nothing about. Or perhaps he will convince you that they are due only to a dietary problem, and that you should seek peace through vitamin supplements or such-like. What one eats is important but should never be worried about; neither should one seek inner peace by solely changing what one consumes. Perhaps the Holy Spirit will lead you to change this, but do not be fooled into thinking that such change alone will bring inner peace. That is Satan diverting you away from the Truth.

THE IMPORTANCE OF
BREATH CONTROL

Both Buddhist and Hindu scriptures, and perhaps others, talk of the importance of controlling one's breathing. Some monks I met in the Himalayas, who follow the Hindu god Shiva and are called 'Saddhus', told me that they have a recommended number of breaths per day. I cannot recall the figure, but it was relatively low. They spend their whole life in meditation and seek to achieve constant awareness of their breathing. Their breathing is as deep, slow and silent as they can make it. The abdomen is pushed out during maximum inspiration and pulled in to expel the final breath in expiration.

Physiologically this can be seen to aid meditation, in that there is evidence to suggest that a natural morphine-like tranquilizer is released in the brain on stretching the covering of the lungs (pleura). This substance is known as endorphine. This theory would explain why runners and others who do vigorous exercises, often describe a feeling of elation, or 'high' afterwards, because they too stretch their lungs to the limit. It would also explain why cigarettes seem to have a calming effect even before the nicotine reaches the brain.

Also, awareness of the rhythm in one's breathing stimulates right brain activity. Increasing any aspect of awareness, as in 'mindfulness' meditation, helps fix one's attention and prevent the mind from wandering into fantasy or nightmare.

I cannot find any direct teaching from Jesus in the Bible to validate this. However, perhaps not all his teachings were recorded, or some were edited out by those who came after him, because they didn't understand and considered them 'quaint but embarrassing eccentricities' in an otherwise wise man.

However, the Gospel of the Essenes, who record Jesus as their Master, has the following to say, (recorded as a quote from Jesus):

'The third communion is with the Angel of Air, who spreads the perfume of sweet-smelling fields, of spring grass after rain, of the opening buds of the Rose of Sharon. We worship the Holy Breath which is placed higher than all the other things created. For, lo, the eternal and sovereign luminous space, where rule the unnumbered stars, is the air we breathe in and the air we breathe out. And in the moment betwixt the breathing in and the breathing out is hidden all the mysteries of the Infinite Garden. Angel of Air, Holy messenger of the Earthly Mother, enter deep within me as the swallow plummets from the sky, that I may know the secrets of the wind and the music of the stars.'

SELF-EXAMINATION
FOR MOTIVE

God doesn't look at what we do in this life. He looks at our motive behind the action. There is no virtue in doing what appears to be great acts of compassion and charity, if the motive behind it is gaining prestige in the community. Thus some people who may appear to be saints on the surface, are inwardly sinners.

Similarly, it is impossible to sin where the motive behind the deed is unconditional love. Despite Jesus' instructions to do otherwise, many of those who call themselves Christians, judge the actions of others. It is not for us to judge others. We do not know the motives behind others' deeds. If we fear that our spiritual brother or sister is doing contrary to God's will, it is right for us to confront him or her, and try to lead him or her back to the true path. This is, of course, providing our motive for doing so is love for him or her.

The more we meditate, the more we become observers of our own thoughts.

The more we observe our own thoughts, the more we become aware of our motives behind our actions. We may become aware of greed, of meanness, or desire for prestige to feed our ego, and then we can stop ourselves from an action fuelled by wrong motive.

For these reasons it is nonsense to live by a book of rules governing actions. As long as our actions and words are motivated by love of God in all His creation, and a desire to do His will; and trust in Him, we can do no wrong.

THE USE AND ABUSE OF DRUGS AND HERBS

God has created a wealth of medical plants, fungi and other substances. Such treasures can be used to heal mind, body and spirit. However, like any of God's gifts, they can be used or abused. The distinction comes on looking at the motive behind the use. No medicinal substance can heal without the God within wishing it so.

Unfortunately, man is vain enough to believe that he can improve on the medicines God gives us. Scientists scorn the use of herbs in healing, but seek prestige through creating chemicals in their laboratories. Such chemical drugs can remove the symptoms of disease and eradicate infections, but they do not heal. Healing is returning the mind, body and soul to wholeness. It is true, though, that drugs can be used to help us over a crisis, and leave us in a state whereby we can commence the healing process. All disease is an inner sign for the need to change. Changes in diet and lifestyle are an obvious need in many sick people. What is less obvious, but often more important, is the need to change one's attitude to life and reasons for living it.

If a doctor cures his or her patient by removing symptoms with drugs or surgery, thereby allowing the patient to continue without change, he or she has done their patient a disservice in the long term. The symptoms of disease are there for a reason; a constant reminder of the need for change within. Obviously,if a doctor's motives for helping a patient over his or her symptom are pure, he or she is doing God's will. However, to heal, i.e. make whole, a patient, that doctor must help the patient gain insight into the root cause of the disease, wherever possible.

Where drugs, or even herbs, are abused to remove symptoms and allow a patient to continue without change, one sees new problems arise in the form of 'side-effects' of the medicine.

Such side-effects are usually much more common and severe with man-made medicines than God-made ones. The active ingredients of God's medicines are balanced by others to avoid or minimize side-effects. The perfection of God's medicines are often missed by the scientist who only sees the 'active ingredient' in a herb, which he extracts, purifies, and claims to have improved on God's gift.

The reason why so many plants and fungi have healing substances within them, often having no use to the plant itself, is an enigma to the heathen scientist. One cannot perceive God by left-brained rationalization alone, and so the poor heathen scientist is left awe-struck and bewildered.

SUBSTANCES AFFECTING MIND AND SOUL

Many people, notably those who consider themselves in authority over others, consider the use of consciousness-altering substances as synonymous with evil. What is more usually the case, is that they consider some consciousness-altering substances as evil, if they don't use them, but condone the use of those that they use, such as alcohol. Such hypocrisy is obvious to all but themselves.

God creates many consciousness-altering herbs and fungi which grow freely amongst every society. Only a fool would suggest that any part of His creation is inherently evil. The evil is in man who abuses His gifts.

Alcohol is the most commonly abused drug in the world, the evil effects of which are plain to see to everybody except alcoholics. Yet Christ himself reputedly took alcohol.

Here then is the difference between use and abuse. There are no reports of Jesus being drunk. Small quantities of alcohol can aid the digestion of meals and facilitate conversation at friendly gatherings. Large quantities of alcohol cause spiritual degeneration with increased aggression, lust, egocentricity.

Alcohol, like other sedating drugs, can be abused to suppress the fears, doubts and guilt which creep into the consciousness of everyone. This permits one to hide from them for a short while. However, if one hides from these, instead of resolving them, they don't go away. They just build up in the sub-conscious to be dealt with later. Abuse of alcohol for this purpose just builds a large bank of fears, doubts, worries, and guilt, deep within you. Each day we have to face these to resolve them, grow stronger, and evolve spiritually. Those who abuse sedating drugs, such as alcohol, heroin and tranquilizers, become spiritually stunted. Because of the build-up of bad thoughts within, when they try to stop taking them, they are overwhelmed. The horrors of having to deal with this build-up leads them to consume more, and so addiction occurs.

It is God's will that we face our fears, doubts and guilt. We are here to overcome them; it is the purpose of our being here. We cannot unite with Him in Heaven until we do. God wants warriors not worriers. When I say 'warriors' I do not mean that He wants aggressive, hate-filled people, I mean that He wants us to be courageous. He wants us to trust Him.

The people who abuse stimulating drugs such as amphetamine, cocaine, 'crack', face a similar problem. These substances cause temporary elation without having to spiritually 'work' for it. Although not tranquilizing, these substances suppress the worries that cause a low mood. Again though, they are not overcome, just buried deep inside to be faced at a later time.

The hallucinogen group of drugs, such as cannabis, 'magic mushrooms', L.S.D., are different in that they don't suppress one's bad thoughts. To some extent they exacerbate them; permit them to come into consciousness. This results in the so called 'bad trip'. Although unpleasant or even terrifying, this experience can be used positively to face our fears, doubt and guilt and resolve them with prayer and meditation. If this isn't done, the 'bad trip' can lead to serious mental and spiritual disturbances.

Hallucinogens have been used as spiritual sacrament in prayer and meditation since the beginning of time. Every culture has references to them, and many cultures outside the West are still using them for this purpose. The Aztecs worshipped magic mushrooms as deities, and called them 'God's flesh'. The Native Church of America, composed largely of American Indians, uses Peyote Cactus, another hallucinogen, which they say Jesus gave to them. The Hindu Saddhus, mentioned earlier, like the Rastafarians, use cannabis, which they smoke all day every day. My meetings with Saddhus in earlier days left me feeling ashamed. While I was rushing around, mind buzzing with thoughts of business, they were sat in meditation radiating inner peace, strength and love. The outward appearance of these 'wild men' is superficially frightening, but their overwhelming gentleness and compassion has to be felt to be believed.

However, not all Saddhus and not all Rastafarians are genuine. Some are just in love with the image and are very far from enlightenment.

Regular use of small quantities of hallucinogens can act as 'psychic purgatives', facilitating the expulsion of bad thought excrement. This is only when they are used with prayer and meditation for the communion with God. Whey they are abused to exacerbate drunkenness, or out of idle curiosity, without any previous spiritual training, the 'bad trip' can lead one to Hell.

This is why historical accounts of hallucinogen experience is so conflicting. Some have said they lead to Hades, or Hell, whilst other have praised their use as a path to God and Heaven. If used with good motives, love in one's heart and trust in God, after first repenting one's sins, to resolve guilt, they can be spiritual growth-promoters. The experience of God's creation during a walk in the country, after taking hallucinogens, is awesome and wonder-filled. Such an experience leads one to perceive the oneness of God's creation; God in everything. If one stops to pray and still the mind in meditation, the lovelight shines forth with ease.

I am not saying that hallucinogens are necessary to experience God or His lovelight. I am saying that they, like everything else, are created by Him for a purpose, and can be used or abused. I am not saying that the hallucinogen experience is for everybody at all stages of their spiritual development.

Clearly many people, particularly in the West, would not benefit from this, at this point in time. One must allow the Holy Spirit to guide one to what one consumes. If, after a period of prayer and meditation one is intuitively led to the experience, one should accept it readily with gratitude for God's gifts, and trust in Him.

DOGS IN THE MANGER

The legal situation concerning God's gift of hallucinogens is designed, through its evil, to distract from the spiritual experience. Those who seek the lovelight with these Keys of Knowledge have first to overcome the paranoia of being a criminal. Possession of a herb can result in imprisonment, disgrace, huge fines, loss of employment, friends and family. These fears are difficult to overcome and all too often, people alter their consciousness with excess alcohol instead. An evil drug condoned by evil societies.

If only man would live by God's laws instead of those dreamt up by other men. If someone tells you something is evil, do not believe him or her, until you have communed with God and verified it. Similarly, if someone tells you something is good or Holy, do not believe until God has verified it in your heart. Include my own writings in this.

To those who consider themselves in authority over others I have the following quotes from the Gospel of Thomas:

'Jesus said: The pharisees and the scribes took the keys of Knowledge, and they hid them. Neither did they enter, nor did they allow to enter those who wished to. But you, become prudent even as serpents and innocent even as doves.'

(Logia 39)

'Jesus said: Woe to them, the pharisees! for they resemble a dog sleeping in the manger of oxen; for neither does he eat nor does he allow the oxen to eat.'

(Logia 102)

A BEHAVIOURAL
VIEWPOINT

Those who study human behaviour can look back to the dawn of our race and see that people of every society in every generation have deliberately tried to alter their consciousness. It appears to be an innate need of human beings. Each of us comes to the realization that this life is not permanent. Life itself comprises a continuous alteration of consciousness, from cradle to grave. We all know we cannot remain in our present state of consciousness forever. As a result we have an innate need to seek other states of consciousness that exist outside of time. We have an inborn desire to seek the timelessness of unity with God. However, God gives us free will. We are free to suppress our inborn programming and cling to this world of desires and self-gratification. However, none of us can cling to it forever. One day we must leave it. Whether we are ready or not is up to us.

DID CHRIST USE OR CONDONE THE USE OF HALLUCINOGENS?

We actually know very little about Christ from what was written about him. However, none of his recorded teachings teach against the use of herbs or fungi for communion. One cannot believe that such a well-travelled man could have not been aware of the presence and use of these. If their use is as evil as the authorities and institutionalized religion's dogma would have us believe, surely he would have specified the point.

John Allegro, in his book *The Sacred Mushroom and the Cross* has speculated that 'magic mushroom' use was common in Christ's time, and that his sacred symbol originated from a mushroom shape. Peter Furst, in his book *Flesh of the Gods*, has looked at the historic use of hallucinogens in all cultures and speculates that the hallucinogenic experience is the root of all religion. He talks about the Shamans, or priest healers, who used hallucinogens in religious rituals. He counts Zarathustra, whose teachings were adopted by the Essene Movement (according to the translator of the Essene gospels, Edmond Bordeaux Szekely) as a Shaman. I quote:

> 'Zarathustra, the founder of Persian religious thought in the sixth century BC, considered himself a shaman, or, as he himself termed it, a psychopomp. According to the Gathas, united in ecstasy with Zarathustra, the dead as well as the living disciples could commune between heaven and earth. Both melotherapy and versotherapy (music and chant) were necessary to the process, which had to occur in a "maga" or enclosed space.'

Why was the enclosed space necessary? To inhale fumes perhaps?

From the same source I quote:

'Sara Bentowa, of the Institute of Anthropological Sciences in Warsaw, has studied the original text of the Old Testament and its Aramaic translation, the *Targum Onculos*, and finds that the word for cane (*kane* or *kene*) appears both alone and linked to the adjective *bosm*, the Hebrew word for aromatic (in Aramaic *busma*). According to the Polish scholar, both *kane bosm* of the Old Testament and the Aramaic *kene busma* refer to Cannabis Sativa.'

He goes on to say:

'A number of traditions developed around the hemp harvest that involved rituals based on intoxication from the volatile resins and oils.'

I am told by an octogenarian friend who has extensively studied the Essenes, that bread was prepared by them in a ritualistic way. The grain was soaked overnight, the water from which was then drunk. The grain was lightly pounded into a flat shape and allowed to dry in the sun. It was not cooked. One wonders if this was to preserve any L.S.D. – containing ergot fungus which is destroyed by high temperatures. Before the advent of fungicides it was common for whole villages to undergo L.S.D. trips from infected bread. St Anthony is reputed to have suffered a 'bad trip' when he was tempted by demons, following ingestion of this fungus.

The hallucinogenic trip only occurs with relatively large doses of hallucinogens. Small quantities are euphoric, giving a sense of joy and well-being. A new generation of anti-depressant drugs used in psychiatry work by raising the levels of a chemical called serotonin in the brain. Both L.S.D. and psylocybin, the hallucinogen in 'magic mushrooms' are structurally almost identical to serotonin.

I suspect that in the future psychiatrists, or psychiatrist/priests, will use hallucinogens both in small doses for their anti-depressant action, and in larger consciousness altering doses to guide patients to insight into the cause of the disease.

This has already been done with L.S.D. in a process known as 'abreaction'. The idea of this therapy is to lead one back to past traumas causing the stress, and then help one come to terms with it, or resolve it. It was abandoned, although occasionally successful, because it was thought to be too unpredictable. Unfortunately it wasn't done with patients properly prepared for the experience by meditation training. Encountering one's fears in a hallucinogenic trip is only therapeutic when one overcomes them by reliving and finding the warmth, and love of God within, i.e. learning to trust Him.

THE OCCULT AND MYSTICISM

To still the mind and find the lovelight within is a mystical experience. Those who achieve such an experience can be known as mystics. Mystics find themselves at a source of awesome power and inner strength. By the practice of meditation, making the two aspects of consciousness unite, and then believing one has power to heal, move mountains, walk on water, or whatever, one *does* have these powers.

I quote from the Gospel of Thomas, logia 48:

'Jesus said: If two make peace with each other in this single house, they will say to the mountain, "Move away" and it shall move.'

However, history is full of evil mystics; those who wield such power to achieve their own selfish ends, or harm others. If one truly believes, one can harm another by casting a spell, performing a ritual or whatever, one can, unless the intended victim protects himself by the greater strength of lovelight. That is, if the victim's faith in God and love is strong, no evil can attack him. God's powers have always been stronger than Satan's.

Jesus warns us that if we choose the path and cast out the demons of the mind, thus achieving the strength of lovelight, and then use that strength for evil, we would end up in a far worse spiritual state than if we had never sought the lovelight. I quote:

'When the unclean spirit has gone out of a man, he passes through waterless places seeking rest; and finding none he says, "I will return to my house from which I came". And when he comes, he finds it swept and put in order. Then he goes and brings seven other spirits more evil than himself, and they enter and dwell there; and the last state of that man becomes worse than the first.'

Should we achieve unity with God's lovelight in meditation, we should never sit back and think we have achieved our goal. Every day of one's life one must struggle with the demons who tempt with vanity, arrogance, ideas of self-esteem and importance. It is one thing to achieve the lovelight experience, it is another to maintain it. Each day one starts anew, casting out the evil from one's mind to allow the lovelight to shine forth. Never give up your vigilance. Never rest on your laurels and think that you have 'made it'.

Do not dabble in astrology. If it is God's will that the future be known to you, He will show you in your path to or from unity with Him in meditation. If God feels it is better for you that you don't know, trust Him in this, as in all matters. If an astrologer tells you good fortune will come your way and you believe it, it will. Similarly, if the astrologer tells you that you will commit evil, or that ill fortune will come your way, that will happen, if you believe. To consult an astrologer is to lay yourself at his or her mercy. Do not allow others to wield such power over you. Trust only in God.

Do not dabble in spiritualism, ouija boards and suchlike. Allow the dead to rest in peace. Those who do are seeking proof in life after death. Trust God and believe. How can you say you truly believe in and trust God if you are continually demanding proof? Do not put the Lord, thy God to the test!

THE WAY OF JOY

Many people see the life of a religious as being boring, dull, unhappy. I, too, had this misconception when I was a drunken, wild-party lover. In those days I experienced great highs of mood and great depths of depression. The life of a religious following Christ's way is different from this. The mood swings seem to even out so that one knows a more even, continual joy that is different from the wild elation of the drunken party-goer. Although everyone goes through times of testing, the religious who knows God does not experience the depths of depression. The lovelight is a continual source of joy and hope for the future. It gives an understanding of life and meaning to its tragedies. I can assure you that the overall experience of life is better as a religious. This is a difficult concept to get over to previous wild-party loving friends who just see me as having become serious and boring.

I quote Jesus from the Gospel of John:
'These things I have spoken to you, that my joy may
be in you, and that your joy may be full.'

LIVING FOR TODAY

The path of meditation is seeking to live in each present moment, unhampered by guilt or resentments from the past or by fears for the future, that are born out of not trusting God. It is impossible to still the mind if there is unresolved guilt which must be repented and released. Trust Jesus when he tells us that God forgives, and think no more of past sins. It is impossible to still the mind if there are resentments and malice disturbing your peace. One must learn to forgive others as well as oneself.

It is impossible to still the mind if one worries about the future. One must trust God and abandon fears and insecurities. So many people spend their lives hoarding money, or paying off massive mortgages so that they may have a secure future. Many of them will not live to see their old age anyway. It is better to live for the day as if it were your last, and be grateful if God grants you more. By living each day as if it were your last, I do not mean one should rape and steal without fear of the consequences. I mean one should be prepared to meet one's Creator and account for one's life, i.e. resolve your conflicts and repent your guilt. I also mean that one should enjoy the beautiful gift of life on a beautiful planet, instead of spending it in fear or anger. I quote Jesus:

> 'Do not be anxious about your life, what you shall eat, nor about your body, what you shall put on. For life is more than food, and the body is more than clothing. Consider the ravens; they neither sow nor reap, they have neither storehouse nor barn, and yet God feeds them. Of how much more value are you than the birds!'
>
> And which of you by being anxious can add a cubit to his span of life? If then you are not able to do as small a thing as that why are you anxious about the rest?
>
> Consider the lilies, how they grow; they neither

toil nor spin; yet I tell you, even Solomon in all his glory was not arrayed like one of these. But if God so clothes the grass which is alive in the field today, and tomorrow is thrown into the oven, how much more will He clothe you, O men of little faith!

And do not seek what you are to eat and what you are to drink, nor be of anxious mind. For all the nations of the world seek these things; and your Father knows that you need them. Instead, seek his kingdom, and these things shall be yours as well.'

My life has held true to Christ's last statement. By not worrying about where I am to live, how I'm going to get money and employment, and seeking God instead, I have still been blessed with all that I have needed. People have said that I am lucky but I do not believe in luck. I have trusted God and tried to do His will, and He has provided for me.

The fact is, when your heart is pure and your mind untroubled, others sense this in you and being attracted by it, give assistance in finding what you need.

OVERCOMING THE DEMON OF IDLENESS

We all have an innate nature to be idle and absorbed into our own world of desires and worries. This must be overcome. It is not possible to find peace in this world whilst we are only taking from it. Giving is an expression of unconditional love which we must find in order to find God's lovelight. Not only does good work distract us from our 'sticky thoughts', it gives us self-respect. To live a life of only taking from the world is to experience guilt and depressive feelings of worthlessness. This is certainly true of the idle 'rich kids' I've met whilst travelling, who devote their life to hedonism; gratifying their selfish desires and getting a sun tan to please their vanity.

One can count travelling as work, if one is working on one's spiritual evolution and helping others do the same. By travelling, one has opportunity to meet others and spread one's beliefs. Share with others your experience; tell them how you have overcome, or are overcoming, the demons of your mind. Listen to their tales and be prepared to learn from them. Never be vain enough to believe that you can only teach and not learn. This was the work Jesus gave his apostles. One can know it is pleasing to God by the peace one wins by it.

By praying for the sick and troubled one meets, one can cure them. This might not happen in your midst but at a later time after you have moved on. People may learn from your words or your example, or both. The seed will be sown for their enlightenment. As long as you have shown them the path they will be able to follow it when they have gathered the strength. Do not expect instantaneous cures or conversions and resulting gratitude and glory to feed your ego. The people you show your lovelight to may well insult you or chase you out of town, but at some point in their lives, even if only on their deathbed, they will remember your example.

Not everyone has the call to travel; not everyone is able to work with their hands or is able to speak healing words. If the only work you are able to do is radiate lovelight to those around you, do not under-estimate its importance or feel that it is any less pleasing in the eyes of God.

I quote Jesus from the Gospel of the Essenes:

'The fifth communion is with the Angel of Work, who sings in the humming of the bee, pausing not in the making of golden honey; in the flute of the shepherd, who sleeps not lest his flock go astray; in the song of the maiden as she lays her head to the spindle. And if you think that these are not as fair in the eyes of the Lord as the loftiest prayers echoed from the highest mountain, then you do indeed err. For the honest work of humble hands is a daily prayer of thanksgiving, and the music of the players is a joyful song unto the Lord. He who eats the bread of idleness must die of hunger, for a field of stones can yield only stones. For him is the day without meaning, and the night a bitter journey of evil dreams. The mind of the idle is full of weeds of discontent; but he who walks with the Angel of Work has within him a field always fertile, where corn and grapes and all manner of sweet-scented herbs and flowers grow in abundance. As ye sow, so shall ye reap. The man of God who has found his task shall not ask any other blessing.'

SECRETS

In logia 6 from the Gospel of Thomas, quoted earlier, Jesus instructs us to become 'prudent even as serpents and innocent as doves'. It is best not to have secrets in one's life. One should be proud of what one is and does, although with humility. One's past evil, if repented, should bring no further shame, and discussion of it with others may help them refrain from similar evil. Certainly we shouldn't concern ourselves with what others think of us. Our peace must depend on what God thinks of us, and Him only.

However, there are times when it is right to withhold information, which is not the same as lying. There are times when prudence and wiliness and needed to lead others to the Truth. Some people need a slow, gentle introduction to the Mysteries. To walk into a room crowded with strangers and suddenly announce that you have found the Path to God, and try to hold a group meditation will, more often than not, cause people to scoff and deride. Perhaps such an action would have a good effect, and if the Holy Spirit moves you to do it, then do it. However, Jesus warns us that prudence is often necesary. Once people have got to know you, and are attracted by the inner peace and lovelight you radiate, one can slowly reveal the Truth, little by little, so as not to disturb them, or have them dismiss you as insane. The latter may well still occur, as it did to Jesus, who not only was declared insane but accused of being Beelzebul, another name for Satan.

However, make sure such prudence is done out of love and desire to spread the Truth, not out of self-doubt or fear of what people may think of you or do to you. There is nothing more pathetic than a closet Christian who believes but is afraid to reveal his or her beliefs. I quote Jesus from the Gospel of Mark:

'Whoever is ashamed of me and of my words, of him will the Son of Man be ashamed when he comes in his glory and the glory of the Father and of the holy angels.'

I too have been guilty of this. It has taken me years to build the courage to write these words. Predictably, they will cause outrage in some, or many, particularly my references to the use of hallucinogens as a sacrament. Howver, the alternative is to live in guilt, and the shame of a coward. I cannot withhold information which may help my spiritual brothers and sisters find the lovelight of God. The past twelve years of my life have shown me all the horrors of alcohol abuse with the accompanying spiritual degeneration, both in myself and others. They have also shown me the terror of the bad trip caused by hallucinogen abuse, but they have also shown me how hallucinogens can be used as a sacrament to find God. Jesus tells us that 'a tree is known by its fruits'. In the past twelve years of experimentation with God-given natural hallucinogens, I have changed from a depressed alcoholic who suffered epileptic fits and anxiety attacks to a humble servant of Jesus Christ who has at last been granted health, joy and inner peace.

I wish to end these writings with a quote from my Master, Jesus, found in the Gospel of the Essenes:

'The fourth communion is with the Angel of Eternal Life, who brings the message of eternity to man. For he who walks with the Angels shall learn to soar above the clouds, and his home shall be in the Eternal Sea where stands the sacred Tree of Life. Do not wait for death to reveal the great mystery; if you know not your Heavenly Father while your feet tread the dusty soil, there shall be naught but shadows for thee in the life that is to come. Here and now is the mystery revealed. Here and now is the curtain lifted. Be not afraid, O man! Lay hold of the wings of the Angel of Eternal Life, and soar into the paths of the stars, the moon, the sun and the endless Light, moving around in their revolving circle for ever, and fly toward the Heavenly Sea of Eternal Life.'

ADDENDUM

FRUITS FROM THE TREE OF LIFE:

You are on a spiritual journey. Turn back at your peril. Go forward, ever changing; living every moment and then forgetting it to live the next. Leap into the abyss with the trust of a small child leaping into the arms of its mother. God loves you. He won't let you fall if you trust Him.

So many conflicting thoughts; spirits and demons pulling both ways; visions of what might be and what might not. And beneath lies calm and Oneness. Need we really do anything else except wait for the situations to present themselves and then ask the Oneness to do His will?

Don't hide from suffering. Embrace it as a lover and ask our Father to glorify His name. Thank Him for the tests He gives you. They are stepping stones en route to Him. Even enlightened men suffer. They don't show it so much because they are outside looking in.

How can you hope to reach God by locking yourselves in man-made boxes? Get outside in His creation. Then move as the Spirit moves you. 'Become a passer-by': JESUS CHRIST – Gospel of Thomas.

To sit and just be; this is feminine, yin, passive. To think and move is masculine, yang, active. The wise man flows in balance, like a butterfly floating between two flowers, letting the air currents decide which he shall visit.

Unless many think you are a fool, you haven't reached wisdom.

Close your eyes. Still your breath and listen to the song of Oneness. Beneath the whispering of trees, the luffing and trickling of water, the chorus of joy from the birds; there you'll find me.

Everything I do, think and say influences the world in which I am. Father, help me find purity – not for my sake but for theirs.

My brother offends me. Let me place his image in mine and lift us both to the Oneness, carried on a wave of love, compassion and forgiveness. Only then can I stop being offended.

Those who consume the Tree of Life shall have their karma speeded past their eyes. They will have strength to bear their burden because they view detached.

We each are a cell in God's huge body; a part of Him but just as a cell contains the genetic blueprint for the whole body, so do our souls contain the whole, or 'oneness' of God.

Worlds within worlds . . . the eternal Word unfolds.

Walk barefoot on the Earth each day – feel the energy flow within you as your Mother reaches up to embrace you with Her love.

Let me be a child of nature. Don't lock me away from my Father and Mother; trapping me with the guilt you instilled. I don't want to be contracted into routine. I don't want debt or insurance policy. Don't you see? I am a bridge between our Father and Mother. You are too. Our Father and Mother commune through me. They can through you too, if you trust and believe.

When the Lovelight shines during conception and gestation, what a generation the next shall be! Not even Satan will bind their spirits. Their courage will know no bounds. How many fears do we learn in the womb?

Another flying dream last night. They always come at time of great testing. God reminds me that I can do anything if only I can but believe. I must never give in to despair. It is no sin to be besieged by the demons of fear and worry. If the demons leave you in peace – they have already claimed your soul. God chastens us to keep us sharp.

No-one knows the Father except he who knows the son. No-one knows God except he who has come to know himself and has overcome the self.

The birthing pains of enlightenment are hard to bear but soon forgotten when the joy of the new born consciousness is beheld. Better experience them now, little by little, than save them all up for the end. In that hell, one second would seem like a million years.

Let the lion lie down with the lamb. Let your strength and courage be balanced by your innocence, gentleness, and purity.

The demons don't like you taking a sacrament, because you seek to drive them out and find the One. They will snap at your heels, but heed not, God will justify you.

Don't hold back your tears. They wash away sins.

God may grant you visions but remember that Satan may also use visions to distract you and lead you from the path. Trust your intuitive feelings about the vision. This is the shepherd's crook guiding you through the narrow gate.

When you reach the Light, feel love, adoration, humility. Trust Him – throw yourself into His arms and beg forgiveness for having been away so long.

The Father says: I have commanded you to transmit love to the world when you think of me. Now I command you to transmit joy, bliss and love to the world.

Never underestimate the demon of gluttony simply because all around you are possessed by it. Meditate while you eat; breathing deep, thanking God with each mouthful and asking Him to bless and purify it. Really chew well each mouthful and concentrate on the taste and texture. The mind is most free from the confines of this particular aspect of the body when you do as Buddha suggests, in keeping your stomach one third full of food, one third full of fluid and one third empty.

The Holy Virgin represents the feminine aspect of God, purity, innocence. She is the lamb aspect of God consciousness. It is She inside you that advocates complete trust in God and 'letting go'. Worship of her pleases God. The man/son of God, Jesus was born from this aspect of God consciousness but possessed in balance also the masculine aspect of God – the strength and courage, represented by the lion.

When these aspects of our own consciousness are developed and balanced, we become true sons and daughters of God.

If you want to change the world, you must change human consciousness, beginning with your own.

If you look into a mirror and see that you are ugly, what good does it do to blame the mirror and smash it?

Why then do you blame sacred plants when they show you what's inside you isn't as it should be. Work on yourself – don't just throw away the mirror so you don't have to see how ugly you are.

GRAFFITI IN RIVERSIDE LODGE, BIRETHANTI, NEPAL:

The swallows fly in the sky,
The water reflects their image,
The swallows leave no traces,
Nor does the water retain their image.

SENEKA '89.

CANNABIS – FOR THE HEALING OF NATIONS

The fact that the illegal herb Cannabis Sativa/Indica is regarded as an aid to the spiritual life, in fact, is a sacrament, to many, is an enigma to Western society as a whole. Its use is regarded to be synonymous with evil by most. Cannabis, or 'Marihuana' as it is sometimes called, has been the subject of social controversy since ancient times: there were those that warned that the hemp plant lined the roads to Hades (or Hell), and those who thought it led to paradise and Heaven. The earliest recorded use is in a Chinese compendium of medicines, the herbal of Emperor Shen Nung, dating from 2737 BC. Its use spread from China to India to North Africa and from there, about AD 1800, to Europe. This introduction came primarily from the troops of Napoleon's army returning from the Egyptian campaign. Although used for centuries in South and Central America, it was not used significantly in the US until about 1920. Since it is a common weed growing freely in many places, there is no way of knowing precisely how extensive is world usage today. A United Nations survey in 1950 estimated that its users then numbered some 200 million people, principally in Asia and Africa. That number must be considerably more today since the widespread adoption of the herb by the young generation of the late 1960's/early 1970's. Many of this generation are still using it, whilst the following generations are also turning to it. With so many users of so many generations it seems unbelievable that mankind has not decided one way or other whether it is useful or detrimental to the spiritual path, or has no effect either way.

Cannabis cannot correctly be described as a drug, as it is in its various forms, still an unrefined plant product. The most common form found in the UK is the resin scraped from the tops of mature plants. This is called 'hashish' and is usually the most refined form available. However, an oil extract is occasionally found, which is the most potent. The drugs contained within Cannabis are manifold, but the main active ingredient is called tetra hydrocannabinol. Isolated chemicals, usually extracted from plants, but nowadays sometimes synthesized in laboratories, are 'drugs'. There is a major distinction to be made here between naturally occurring, God given, plants and chemical substances which are never found alone in nature but which man has produced in a vain attempt to better that which is created. When man creates drugs from herbs he usually produces a substance which is much more potent, in the short term, and quicker acting, but with pronounced toxic side effects, particularly with long term usage. These are usually absent in all but a few herbal remedies unless taken in very large dosage. This is because God creates His medicines in a form that is perfectly balanced, with many other substances not only diluting the active ingredient or drug, but actively opposing unwanted effects.

I personally have only once heard of someone taking the drug tetrahydrocannabinol. A young doctor friend, who was not unused to cannabis, told me that he had 'snorted' this whilst studying in Canada alongside a fellow medical student. He told me that they both underwent a three day nightmare of confusion and anxiety. I mention this to emphasize that there is a difference between drug taking and herb taking.

The concept of plants and fungi being sacred, and their consumption aiding one to find God through devotional practices, is as old as mankind itself. Some anthropologists believe that the root of mankind's religions lie in experiences induced by ingestion of hallucinogens. Hallucinogens are substances which alter perception rather than induce true 'hallucinations', which are rare, even in psychiatric wards. A true hallucination occurs when one perceives an object, sound or tactile sensation whilst there is nothing physical to cause it. What tends to occur with hallucinogens is that one perceives incoming sensory data in an altered way. For instance, one might become riveted by the beauty of a plant or scene which under normal circumstances would seem quite ordinary. In fact, enhancement of one's appreciation of beauty, particularly natural beauty, is an almost universal phenomenon, as is enhancement of music appreciation, amongst hallucinogen users.

From this point of view, the term 'hallucinogen' is a misnomer, although true hallucinations can occur with very large doses of true hallucinogens, such as L.S.D. and 'magic mushrooms'. Although many pharmacology books list cannabis as a hallucinogen it is recognized as being markedly different to the others in character, and much less likely to cause true hallucinations. What all these substances can do is induce 'visions' with one's eyes closed, particularly when one is in a relaxed contemplative/meditative mood. At such a time one may seem to be transported to a non-physical, spiritual world, which can be exquisite beyond words, or terrifying, depending on one's current mental state. It is my personal belief that this experience is potentially healing and would, if pursued by the majority of our race, cause a radical change in attitudes towards life and reasons for living it, which would be conducive to planetary survival and in line with God's will. For this reason I think that cannabis might be the tree of life mentioned in the Biblical book of prophecy Revelations. '. . . and the leaves of the tree were for the healing of nations.' Chapter 22, verse 2. This has long been thought to be the case by the Rastafarians.

Most people, I'm sure, would believe that taking cannabis is harmful to one's health. However, herbal pharmacopoeias of many cultures describe its medicinal virtues, and have done for millenia. *The Illustrated Book of Herbs*, Octopus Books, for instance lists its properties as being sedative, analgesic and antispasmodic and hence of use in treating insomnia, depression, neuralgia, migraine, asthma and as a local anaesthetic in dentistry.

Religious and Useful Plants of Nepal and India, by Prof. Trilok Chandra Majupuria, has the following to say concerning the medicinal effects of cannabis: It serves as a remedy for malaria, black water fever, blood poisoning. Leaves are sedative, anodyne, narcotic, antispasmodic, diuretic, digestive and astringent, and are good for diarrhoea and dysentery. Leaves induce sleep and are also used in tetanus and for relieving pain. Leaves are boiled before use and are also used externally for removing dandruff and vermin, pain in ear, for dressing fresh wounds and sores. Poultice of fresh leaves is used for piles and orchitis. 'It is prescribed in dyspepsia, gonorrhoea, bowel complaints, appetizer and nervine stimulant.' 'Very useful for

80

inducing sleep in those who suffer hallucinations.' It describes hashish as being 'useful in malarial and periodical headache, anaemia, nervous vomiting, tetanus, convulsion, insanity, delirium, nervous exhaustion. It is used as aphrodisiac.'

However, the professor has written even more fascinating material on the religious aspect of cannabis. (From the Hindu point of view):

'It is said that Lord Shiva, one of the trinity of Hindu deities, found the Bhang plant (Cannabis Sativa) a choice plant. So the Hindu devotees regard him the "Bangeri Baba" i.e. the god who prefers heartily the enjoyment of Bhang and is often under the impact of Bhang and consequently in the oblivious state of the outer surroundings. So even the devotees heartily like the plant and enjoy the drink prepared from its dried seeds to be transported to the seventh bliss of heaven. And one can come cross the ascetics in number who practise meditation preferring this plant.' He goes on to say:

'There are several references to this plant under the name of Vijaya in religious literature. It is mentioned that during the churning of the ocean this plant appeared. At the time of the Shivaratri festival which is celebrated in honour of Lord Shiva and which falls in the month of Falgun (February-March) it is considered that Shiva blesses his devotee. Under the intoxication of this plant, the persons become interested to win the whole Universe.'

A very comprehensive review of the effects of cannabis on the body and mind is to be found in the Scientific American magazine, December 1969, written by Lester Grinspoon. I quote 'There is a substantial body of evidence that moderate use of marihuana does not produce physical or mental deterioration.' He quotes many extensive scientific studies and quotes psychiatrists Samuel Allentuck and K.H. Bowman who, after extensive studies, said 'marihuana will not produce psychosis (loss of contact with reality) de novo in a well-integrated, stable person.' He goes on to say 'This is not to say that the drug may not precipitate an acute anxiety state with paranoid thoughts or even a temporary psychosis in a susceptible person. A drug that alters the state of consciousness and distorts perception and the body image may well tip a delicately balanced ego, already overburdened with anxiety, into a schizophrenic reaction.'

Thus he is saying that if one is on the verge of madness, cannabis might potentially tip one over the edge. I believe this to be true as cannabis 'opens the flood gates' of the subconscious. The great bank of psychic excrement; the sticky thoughts mentioned before, if allowed to surge into the conscious mind without having had the necessary training in meditation and prayer, may well overwhelm one.

However, the point is that if one can regularly allow the psychic excrement into consciousness and deal with it, one can mature spiritually and emotionally at an increased rate. Mr Grinspoon goes on to say 'Very little research attention has been given to the possibility that marihuana might protect some people from psychosis. Among users of the drug the proportion of people with neuroses or personality disorders is usually higher than in the general population; one might therefore expect the incidence of psychosis also to be higher in this group. The fact that it is not suggests that for some mentally disturbed people the escape provided by the drug may serve to prevent a psychotic breakdown.'

The fact that one finds a greater incidence of minor mental disturbance in cannabis smokers is hardly surprising. Drugs of all kinds are used by sick people in an attempt to cure themselves. This does not mean that it is necessarily the drug that is making them sick. Could it be that the God within (Holy Spirit) is leading these disturbed people to the cannabis experience? Even if they do experience the hell of temporary anxiety, paranoia or psychosis, this experience may benefit them spiritually in the long run. Hell-like experiences in this life make one doubly sure that one doesn't want to experience them for all eternity in the next. And if cannabis users learnt to deal with the psychic excrement causing the 'bad trips', i.e. overcome their selves, with all the inherent fear, doubts, greed, desires, etc. attached to those 'selves', by the contemplative path of prayer and meditation, God may well heal them with this herb.

I personally believe that man is currently undergoing an awakening process. He is gradually realizing that what he consumes affects consciousness much more than he first thought. For this reason mankind will replace alcohol with cannabis, as the prime substance for altering consciousness. Similarly, he will replace his diet of putrefying dead animal flesh and other sources of animal protein not intended for our consumption, with pure organically grown, unrefined vegetable matter. Both of these steps will lead to improved physical, mental and spiritual health in our race. Aggression will become a thing of the past. We will return, in time, to mankind's state before 'the Fall' i.e. we will return to a state of consciousness we knew in Paradise.

In my research of recent nutritional literature the only good thing I can find in consuming animal products, is that animal fats protect one's liver from alcoholic liver disease. (Vegetarian and vegan alcoholics beware!) A possible scenario for the Fall of mankind emerges. Instead of spending their lives appreciating the wonders and beauty of Paradise, i.e. using their right brains, our early ancestors delved into left brain thinking to improve and increase production of alcohol. (Remember that small amounts of alcohol naturally occur in the juices of rotting fruits.) The increased consumption of alcohol led men to intuitively seek out a diet high in animal fats to protect his liver. The change in diet, together with the alcohol, caused mankind to lose his inherent access to God-consciousness and enter Hell-like states which lead to aggression, murder, selfishness and all the other evils that currently make us lower than animals. When humans came to be born from the wombs of mothers undergoing these Hell-like states, (and from the seed of fathers in similar state), human 'nature' as we know it, became self-perpetuating.

Those whose favourite retort is 'Ah, but Jesus ate flesh', should read John Wynne-Tyson's book *Food for a Future*. He gives excellent quotes from Apocryphal sources to suggest otherwise. He also explains how the whole world's population may be adequately fed, with no need for starvation at all, by mankind's change in diet. (It takes seven tons of grain to produce one ton of meat.)

Why is it then that world governments are so determinedly trying to stamp out use of cannabis? Grinspoon comes close to the answer when he says 'Marihuana's effects in producing a state of introspection and bodily passivity is repellent to a cultural tradition that prizes activity, aggressiveness and achievement. And it may well be that social prejudices enter into the public alarm concerning the drug: prejudice on the part of the older generation, which sees marihuana as a symbol of the alienation of the young, and on the part of the white population, which, perhaps largely unconsciously, regards marihuana as a non-white drug that is rapidly invading the white community, because until recently the smoking of marihuana took place mainly in the ghettoes of Negroes, Puerto Ricans and people of Mexican origin.'

Let us also remember the vast, vast quantities of revenue produced by alcohol taxation. It would be difficult for governments to tax a weed that grows freely in anyone's greenhouse or windowsill.

SUGGESTED FURTHER READING LIST:
(although I do not necessarily agree with all that is contained)

The Gospel of Thomas – presented by Hugh McGregor Ross
Jesus – Essential Readings. New Testament and Apocryphal teachings attributed to Jesus. Edited and Introduced by Anthony Duncan.
The Imitation of Christ by Thomas à Kempis.
The Cloud of Unknowing – translated by Clifton Wolters – written by anonymous fourteenth century author.
Meister Eckhart Sermons and Treatises, translated and edited by M.C.C. Walshe.
Altered States of Awareness – readings from *The Scientific* American magazine – various authors.
Doors of Preception/Heaven and Hell by Aldous Huxley.
Siddhartha by Hermann Hesse.
Shambhala – the Sacred Path of the Warrior by Chogyam Trungpa.
The Diamond Healing – Tibetan Buddhist Medicine and Psychiatry by Terry Clifford.
Yoga – McDonald Guidelines series.
Jesus lived in India – Holger Kersten.
Religious and Useful Plants of Nepal and India by Trilok Chandra Majpuria (Professor of Tribhuvan University, Kathmandu), revised by D.P. Joshj.
The Acorn Book of Healing Through Christ Consciousness – various contributors – Acorn Publishing.
Terra Christa by Ken Carey.
Avalon Arise, Acorn Book 2 – various contributors, Acorn Publishing.
The Tao of Physics by Fritjof Capra.
The Awakened Mind – Maxwell-Cade and Coxhead
The Yoga of the Christ in the Gospel According to St John by Ravi Ravindra.